"PICKLE PIE"

By Seth and Tanika Warden

Illustrated by Kara Kniffen

Management and Production: Tanika Warden

Layout and design by Dan Castle at Creative Artist Productions.

Lyrics used from "Pickle Pie", on the 2011 release "Hi, Hello, How do you do?" by "Seth and the Moody Melix"

Pickle Pie Productions, LLC
PO Box 2424
Wilton NY, 12831
www.picklepieproductions.com

This book is dedicated to our daughters Ella and Aria. You have brought such inspiration and joy to our lives and this book is the proof. We love you both so much. Thank you to my wife Tanika for believing my dream and supporting me every step of the way. Without your help, this book wouldn't be here today.
I love you always.

Printed in the United States of America

When I was
sitting in
a diner

down in
South Carolina,

something
sweet and sour

Desserts

Keylime Pie..... $1.75

Pickle Pie..... $1.50

Chocolate Pie..... $2.00

caught my eye.

This little
old lady

asked me what I'd like to try,

I'd like a piece
of pickle pie!

Pickle Pie,

Pickle Pie,

Pickle Pie,

Pickle Pie

there's nothing
   more that I would like to try!

This little old lady
asked me what
I'd like to try,

I'd like a
piece of
pickle pie!

When I was sitting
in a cafe,

somewhere
over that way,

something
sweet and sour

caught my eye.

**There was a
merry little man**

**with a cheesecake
in his hand,**

he asked me

if I'd like a slice.

I said thank you
very kindly, but there's something
else behind me

that I would
really like to try.

Said the merry little man, with the cheesecake in his hand,

"Would you
like a piece

of pickle pie?"

Pickle Pie,

Pickle Pie,

Pickle Pie,

Pickle Pie

there's nothing
more that I would like
to try!

Said the merry little man,
with the cheesecake
in his hand,

"Would you like
a piece of
pickle pie?"

PICKLE PIE

2 eggs
3/4 tsp corn starch
1/2 tsp cinnamon
1/2 cup light cream
6 oz sweet pickles (ground)
1 cups sugar
1 Tbsp of butter
1/2 tsp nutmeg
1/2 tsp lemon extract

Meringue Topping

3 eggs beaten
1/8 tsp salt
5 Tbsp sugar
1/8 tsp lemon juice
& green food color

Bake at 350 degrees for
1 hour then apply topping.

Recipe yields one pie.

* For a sweeter taste, add a layer of chocolate brownie mix
to the crust then add filling and meringue topping.

PICKLE PIE

As recorded by Seth and the Moody Melix

(From the 2011 Album HI, HELLO, HOW DO YOU DO?)

Words and Music by Seth Warden
Arranged by Seth Warden

B7

E

♩ = 110
Gtr I When I was Sit-ting in a diner down in south ca - ro - li - na something sweet and sour caught my eye, this
Gtr I little old lady asked me what I'd like to try, I'd like a piece of pi - ckle pie. Pi - ckle pie pi - ckle
Gtr I pie, there's nothing more that I would like to try this lit - tle old la - dy asked me
Gtr I what I'd like to try, I'd like a piece of pi - ckle pie!
Gtr I When I was sit - ting in a ca - fe, somewhere over that way something sweet and sour caught my
T
A
B

24
Gtr I eye, there was a merry little man with a cheesecake in his hand, he asked me if I'd like a slice I said
TAB
29
Gtr I thank you very kindly but theres something else behind me, that i would really like to try said the
TAB
33
Gtr I merry little man with the cheesecake in his hand, would you like a piece of pi - ckle pie? pi - ckle pie pi - ckle
TAB
38
Gtr I pie there's nothing more that I would like to try said the merry little man with the
TAB
42
Gtr I cheesecake in his hand, would you like a piece of pi - ckle pie? Pi - ckle pie pi - ckle
TAB

Gtr I pie   there's nothing more that I would like to   try   said the   merry   little   man   with the

rit.

Gtr I cheesecake in his hand   would you   like   a   piece of   pi - ckle   pie?

www.ingramcontent.com/pod-product-compliance
Lightning Source LLC
Chambersburg PA
CBHW041237040426
42445CB00004B/56